Melieron's Magic

DOUGLAS HILL

Illustrated by Steve Hutton

For my grandson
EOIN
and again for Rose

PACIFIC
L E A R N I N G

05 04 03 02 01
10 9 8 7 6 5 4 3 2 1

Published by
Pacific Learning
P.O. Box 2723
Huntington Beach, CA 92647-0723
www.pacificlearning.com

ISBN: 1-59055-094-3

PL-7601

Contents

Land of the
The Greenwood

Stonewall
Foothills

the Peaceful

Western
Grassland

MONSTERS

← THE VALLEY

FOOTHILLS

Saelez's Cave

MOUNTAINS

Forest

Melleron's Cottage

<Village>

FARMLANDS

CHAPTER 1

Dark Powers

The high meadow led to the base of a ridge, a slope of coarse grass, and crumbling rock. Farther up, the slope rose more steeply into a forbidding stone wall, where once there had been a dark opening leading into a cave.

This opening had recently and mysteriously disappeared, like a healed wound.

Yet the space of the cave itself still existed, hidden behind the surface of the stone.

The space itself was greatly changed – lights brightened it, furnishings and carpets and hangings hid its dank walls and dirt floor.

At the center of the cave, hunched in a large, carved chair, a man in a hooded purple cloak was practicing magic.

Staring with glittering eyes at a tapestry on one wall, he lifted a skinny hand and muttered a stream of words. The tapestry immediately started shimmering – but its bright patterns remained unchanged.

The hooded man scowled at it. "Move, blast it!" he snarled.

He looked down at an open book resting on his lap – small but incredibly thick and crammed with unreadably tiny writing. Yet when he touched a page, the writing suddenly enlarged. Peering closely, he nodded. "There," he muttered. "I overlooked that..."

He repeated the words, while moving one hand in a spiral motion. The patterns in the tapestry began to swirl and writhe, while the cloth flapped and fluttered.

As the hooded man smiled in satisfaction, a large shaggy mass stirred at the back of the cave and rose to its feet. It was a monstrous creature, covered in thick black hair, with yellow eyes glowing in the flickering light.

"Are you still fooling with that?" the monster growled in a deep hoarse voice.

"I'm not fooling," the hooded man snapped, closing the book. "I'm simply improving my surroundings."

The hairy one yawned, fangs glinting. "Why? I thought you were leaving soon."

"While I'm here," the hooded one said stiffly, "I want it to be pleasant."

The hairy one grunted impatiently. "Well, I want to do something besides watch you decorate a cave. I may visit my homeland..."

"No," the hooded one interrupted. "That would be an unnecessary risk."

"You do not tell me no," the hairy one rumbled. "I do what I want."

The hooded one glared at him. "Are you going to endanger our plans just because you're bored?" Rising, he tucked the thick book carefully into his cloak. "As it happens, I think we should now be able to go back to the forest. It's been over a month, and everything should have settled down…"

"It's about time!" the hairy one said, baring his fangs in a grin. "So we can finally punish those two little pests!"

"Indeed," the hooded one hissed, "and in ways that will benefit us both. We'll find the boy too and teach him what it means to serve me."

Meanwhile, far away from that hidden cave, two small beings were fleeing for their lives.

One bounded on four sturdy legs, the other soared on delicate wings, as they fled across an eerie plain, barren and deathly beneath a pale moon. Racing close behind them were two pursuers.

The first was huge, yellow-eyed, and shaggy. It had fangs and claws and horns glinting in the moonlight. The second was a shadowy figure in a hooded cloak, sailing through the air, bony hands reaching out...

The pursuit was being watched from a nearby hilltop by a boy of about twelve years old, who was small, thin, and dark-haired. His face was twisting, his body quivering as if he wanted to leap down from the hilltop, but something held him still.

The two small ones were losing that ghastly race, and their pursuers drew ever closer.

Then, despairingly, the winged one looked toward him, and shrieked his name – perhaps it was a hopeless cry for help, or perhaps an anguished farewell.

"Melleron! Melleron!"

CHAPTER 2

Shadow of Fear

Melleron woke with a jolt that almost threw him out of bed, and saw his white-haired grandmother, his Nan – who had been calling him – in the doorway.

"Are you all right, Melleron?" Nan said anxiously. "You were moaning…"

"I'm fine," he mumbled, shivering with a leftover chill from the nightmare. "I just had a bad dream…"

Nan relaxed. "I thought it was a stomachache or worse. Never mind, there's sunshine and breakfast to chase away bad dreams."

Leaping up, quickly washing and dressing, Melleron dashed to the kitchen where Nan was waiting with hot pancakes. Still, the nightmare, which had troubled him several times before, left a shadow on his mind.

"Nan," he said, swallowing the last bite of his third pancake, "do dreams ever show what's going to happen?"

"Some folk think they do," the old woman said, "but I doubt it. Dreams are too muddled and unreal. I reckon if they mean anything at all, they tell what might be troubling us." She patted Melleron's hand. "I'm not surprised you're still having nightmares, after what happened not much more than a month ago."

That helped to push away the shadow of Melleron's dream, and so did working on the everyday chores around the cottage during the morning. Around noon, because it was a humid day in high summer, Nan decided to stop and rest in the shade a while.

This left Melleron free to dash away toward the place he loved best of all – the enormous, wild expanse of the Peaceful Forest.

He didn't have far to go, as the cottage stood within the fringes of the forest. He felt no unease about plunging alone into its shadowy depths. Both of his grandparents had been skilled foresters – Nan still was, although she had grown a bit shaky – and had taught Melleron a forester's skills, to keep him safe.

Also, the forest held few dangers, for long ago all its dangerous beasts had been cleared out permanently. It had happened almost by accident, when people fought and won a war against an army of terrible beings from the Stonewall Mountains during the Monster War.

As Melleron trotted along a familiar forest path, he wasn't thinking about that ancient battle. Instead he was remembering his nightmare, and its cause. For it came from a time, a month or so before, when he and two unusual friends had fought a small frightful war of their own in the forest.

Their enemy had been a huge, hairy, ferocious monster named Horrimal, who had come over the mountains to raid and terrorize the human lands. In the Peaceful Forest, Horrimal had threatened Melleron's two friends, and Melleron was caught up with them in deadly danger. Even worse, Horrimal had an ally, an evil magician named Saelez, who had wanted to imprison Melleron.

Somehow, with courage and cleverness and luck, Melleron and his friends had managed to defeat their enemies. Horrimal and Saelez fled, and the forest was peaceful again.

16

In fact, life in general had been better since then for Melleron. Before that, he and Nan had been quite poor, and were scorned or ignored by most people in the area. But after Horrimal had been driven off, the grateful people raised a large sum of money for Melleron as a reward. Even better, everyone had grown much friendlier.

So, Melleron thought, this amazing summer was turning out to be nearly perfect – except for the nightmare he kept having.

Well, also except for the fact that the monster Horrimal and the magician Saelez were still lurking somewhere in the Stonewall Mountains, north of the forest.

No doubt they were full of hatred and fury, and possibly plotting revenge...

Yet Melleron seemed to be the only one thinking about that, just as he was the only one having nightmares. Even his two friends, even Nan, seemed to believe that the monster and the magician had gone for good, and there was nothing more to worry about.

"But they could still come back..." Melleron muttered to himself, on the forest path.

Then he almost jumped out of his shoes when, with a rustle of twigs, something sprang at him from a thicket while something else whirled down from above.

CHAPTER 3

Shattered Peace

The first of these mysterious somethings looked like a living statue – a sturdy little dog, but made of hard stone. The second had the wings, claws, and scales of a dragon, but was no bigger than a bush-pigeon, and was a bright, startling pink.

"Are you talking to yourself, Melleron?" the dragon laughed. Her name was Rose, which she insisted was her color, too, as she hated the word "pink."

"I'm just thinking out loud," Melleron said. "I had the dream again, about you two being chased by Horrimal and Saelez."

"Rrrrr," said the little dog, whose name was Grit. He bared sharp teeth that were actually diamonds. He understood what they said, but just spoke his own language, so only Rose understood him.

"Grit says you should dream about *us* chasing *them*," Rose told Melleron.

"I don't want to dream about them at all," Melleron muttered. "I keep wondering if the dream is some sort of warning."

"A dream is just a dream – pictures in the night," Rose said firmly. "Those two are a long way away from here."

Melleron sighed. "What about your idea of telling the chief of the monsters what happened? He might do something – about Horrimal, anyway."

Rose waved a wing. "I may do that, sometime, although I don't think the chief cares what happens here. Most monsters don't. Anyway, they're not likely to hunt for Horrimal."

"Rrrr," Grit said. "Rrrr."

Rose nodded. "Grit says, why ruin the summer worrying?"

He's right, Melleron thought. Especially such an amazing summer, with the three of them together amid the ever-changing marvels of the forest. Autumn, and the re-opening of the village school, would arrive all too soon.

Firmly, he pushed away his worries. "What do you want to do?" he asked brightly. "Go back to that vale we were exploring, or find something to eat?"

"Rrrr!" Grit said, wagging a stumpy tail.

"Eat!" Rose cried, swirling into the air.

They set off toward one of Rose's favorite places, a grove of silverberry bushes, which always had ripe fruit on their branches any time of year. Along the way they paused by an outcrop of flinty rock, which was Grit's favorite place. He was made of stone and he ate stone – and he always enjoyed a nice chunk of flint.

When he had broken off a big piece with his diamond teeth, they went on to the silverberry grove, where Melleron and Rose gobbled the big juicy berries while Grit gnawed his flint like a dog with a bone. After that, they went wandering through the wonderful forest.

They watched harelings playing, striped ducks paddling, swarm-beetles marching. They startled a little bushcat, which Grit chased up a cherrynut tree, just for fun. As usual, they visited a clearing where an ancient iron-oak tree lay uprooted, and where they watered a tiny seedling that had sprouted among the torn-up roots of its mighty ancestor.

At last, as the afternoon shaded into evening, it was time for Melleron to set off for home. There was a heavy gathering of thunderclouds, tinged red by the sunset as if wounded, growling distantly as if in pain.

The clouds were still overhead the next morning, like a stifling weight upon the humid forest. Melleron shrugged off the gloom and went to meet his friends again.

He couldn't find them.

Wondering what had delayed or distracted them, he searched around their usual places, while the clouds grumbled overhead. Still they didn't appear. At midday the storm attacked with torrents of rain, lightning lancing through the gloom. For Melleron, sheltering under a goldfir tree, the rain was the least of his concerns.

Rose and Grit had never before failed to meet him. Also, rain never bothered them.

So... where were they?

When the downpour stopped and the storm drifted away, Melleron went back to searching, ranging more widely, calling their names. After another hour or two he fell silent, moving with a forester's quiet step – while within him puzzlement gave way to anxiety, and finally to dread.

By then, ranging into the northern reaches of the forest, he was aware of a weird feeling all around. The forest had grown still, with an unnatural stillness, as if its creatures were holding their breath, silenced by terror. Melleron had known that feeling before – when the monstrous Horrimal had prowled the forest's shadows...

It can't be him, Melleron tried to tell himself. It must be something else...

Despite his most positive thoughts, a coldness like ice crystals gathered along his spine, even in the humid heat.

Soon he was toiling up a low hill tangled with wirethorn and hookweed, where the stillness felt heavy, as if the very air was gripped by fright. On the crest of the hill he looked across a sweep of open ground, mostly free of trees. There he saw a scene that was his nightmare come true.

On the far side of that open area, Rose and Grit were fighting a hopeless, losing battle against their most deadly enemies.

CHAPTER 4

Wrong over Right

Fearless as ever, Grit was leaping and snapping at the monster Horrimal while Rose flew and clawed at the monster's frightful face. Horrimal, growling like the departed thunder, was kicking savagely at Grit and swatting at Rose.

At the same time the magician Saelez was hopping around them, yelling. Lengths of weirdly glowing rope were leaping magically from his hands, seeking to wrap around Rose and Grit. They were quick and agile enough, however, to dodge both the ropes and the sweeping blows of the monster.

In the midst of the battle Saelez reached into his cloak and brought out a small, thick book. After glancing at a page, the magician lifted his glittering gaze.

"Careful!" he shouted at Horrimal, as the monster slashed furiously at Rose. "Don't damage that pink skin!"

Instantly Rose whirled. "Not pink!" she shrieked. "Don't call me pink!" A blazing stream of blue fire erupted from her mouth.

She hadn't yet breathed dragon-fire during the battle, because she could never do it when she wanted to. It burst out only when she grew completely berserk with fury.

Fighting Horrimal merely made her fiercely angry, but the hated word "pink" threw her over the edge into an almost crazed, truly blazing rage.

Screeching with shock, Saelez reeled back, thrusting the book into his cloak. Then he shouted a few strange words – and more lengths of the magical rope appeared out of thin air, and wove themselves into a glowing net.

The net immediately wrapped around Rose, one strand looping around her mouth to stifle her flame. As she fell, struggling and raging, Saelez flung another net around Grit, its magic withstanding his strength and his sharp diamond teeth.

Side by side on the grass the two of them lay, helpless, as Horrimal's huge clawed hands reached down to them.

At this, Melleron leaped from the hilltop in a wild, desperate charge.

He had no chance against Horrimal or Saelez, but he simply couldn't stand there while Rose and Grit were trussed up and taken captive. He hadn't reached them, however, when Horrimal picked up the two prisoners and galloped heavily away into the forest. Then Saelez, with more words of magic, was suddenly transformed into the winged shape of a swallow-hawk, which flashed away among the treetops.

Melleron was left standing there alone on that open ground, as if he were rooted, pale and trembling. Around him the forest creatures returned to their everyday sounds, as if nothing had happened there at all.

Melleron took a step forward, thinking wildly that he might track Horrimal through the forest, hoping to find some way to help... Then he whirled fearfully at the sound of a rustle behind him.

He stared in bewilderment at the sight of his grandmother, hobbling toward him.

"Melleron..." she gasped.

"Nan!" he said. "What are you doing here?"

"I've been looking for you..." she said, moving closer.

Melleron was disturbed to see that she looked much shakier than normal – pale and weak and hollow-eyed. "What's wrong, Nan?" he asked worriedly. "Are you sick?"

"The heat..." she croaked, reaching a trembling hand toward him. "I think I've walked too far..."

As Melleron hurried to support her, she let her hand fall on his arm. Its grip was strangely firm, despite her weakness. Also, her hair seemed longer and wilder than usual, she was wearing a dark dress he had never seen before, and her eyes seemed to be glittering...

Just as he put all those details together, it became too late.

The old woman shimmered – and became Saelez the magician, laughing cruelly, clutching Melleron's arm.

CHAPTER 5

Into Captivity

"I did well imitating the old crone, didn't I?" Saelez cackled. "Despite the fact that I only saw her once, a month ago!"

Terrified, Melleron fought to free himself. Saelez snarled some harsh words – and another glowing magic net wrapped itself around him.

Just then Horrimal crashed back into the clearing, with Rose and Grit still in his clutches.

"Why did you call me back... ?" Horrimal began. Then he saw Melleron, and his scowl became a savage grin. "The boy!" he growled. "How did you find him?"

"He just came running along," Saelez smirked. "I saw him from the air. Perhaps he thought he could help his little friends."

Horrimal grunted. "I suppose you want me to carry them all."

"No, no," Saelez said airily. "I can take the dragon. She weighs no more than a small bird." His laughter rasped. "I thought I'd have to search for the boy – but instead he has come to me, as if he wants to be my slave!"

Horrimal scooped up Melleron and Grit, and galloped into the forest again, a captive under each arm. For Melleron, it brought back a time once before when he was carried off, half-stifled by the monster's matted hair. Around that hairy neck, as before, he saw a green stone on a chain, like a pendant – a magic stone, that Saelez used to speak to Horrimal from afar.

For some reason, Melleron seemed to be aware of things – the stone, the monster's rank smell, the glowing net – as if from a distance. In his horror and despair he slid into an empty numbness that settled on him like a fog.

During that first terrible day, Melleron's mind was mostly blank. He scarcely felt the ache from Horrimal's grip, or the jolting as the monster loped on over the rough wild land. He hardly noticed when at last they left the forest, starting up across the rugged foothills leading to the Stonewall Mountains. The passage of time itself barely registered on his numbed mind, as that nightmare journey went on and on.

Through it all, the monster seemed untroubled by his burdens. Though he was heavy-footed and far from swift, his pace never slackened, no matter how steep the slope, how rough the footing. By sunset he entered a deep ravine, a shadowed gap between cliffs that formed a corridor through the mountains. Even its darkness failed to slow down Horrimal.

Then, at last, beyond the ravine, Horrimal came to a halt, and set down his captives. The sudden release – from the monster's grip and the endless movement – jerked Melleron partway back toward awareness. It was also possible that after so many long hours, the effects of shock and terror were beginning to wear off, and his numbing inner fog to lift a little.

He noticed that Grit had somehow wriggled one paw free from the magic net. When Horrimal turned away from them, Grit growled softly and intensely, and reached over to touch Melleron with that paw, its claws like splinters of granite.

In that moment even more of Melleron's clouded blankness fell away.

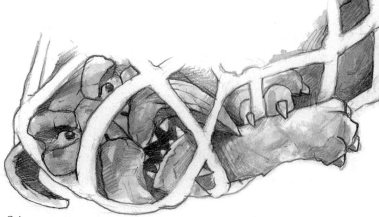

He could see the little dog's unflinching courage flaring in his eyes, and he realized that Grit was wordlessly urging him not to be crushed by terror and hopelessness – not to let himself give in, or give up.

Slowly Melleron nodded, clutching at whatever shreds of his own courage he could find. "All right, Grit," he croaked. "I'll be all right. Don't worry…"

Then he gasped and went still. Horrimal loomed over them, and scooped them up, but he merely took them to a stream at the edge of the gully, and held their faces down to the icy water so they could drink. He had also found some wild flat-peas, and roughly fed a few to Melleron while Grit gnawed at a flinty pebble.

Melleron slept little during the chill mountain night, and felt stiff and exhausted when Horrimal hoisted them up at daybreak and set off again. At least he was aware of the feeling, and was no longer lost in that terrible, empty blankness – although that second day made him almost long for it again. The hours passed with agonizing slowness, as Horrimal climbed across one gravel-covered slope and narrow ledge and bumpy crest after another. In the end, even Grit was silenced by misery.

Then – with startling suddenness – the journey ended.

Horrimal was shambling across a high meadow, toward another rocky ridge, when a patch of the ridge's bare stone suddenly shimmered, then opened, like a mouth. It was the mouth of a cave, and Saelez stood in it.

"Welcome," the magician said with a cackling laugh as Horrimal climbed up into the cave and set his captives down. "I'm glad you've arrived safely."

Melleron ignored him, twisting within the net, peering around at the cave's weird and unexpected furnishings, and trying to see Rose.

"Looking for a way out?" Saelez laughed. "Don't bother. We may soon live in a far finer place than this, but you will be in my power there as you are here. Believe me, boy – for you, there is no escape."

CHAPTER 6

Magician's Cave

Turning away, Saelez murmured a word, and the cave mouth vanished again. Though the cave was lit by gleaming spheres, to Melleron the loss of the daylight was like the closing of a tomb.

Horrimal lumbered over to a mat at one side. "Keep them quiet," he rumbled. "I need some rest after that journey." He settled into a shaggy mass and almost at once began snoring.

Saelez beckoned to Melleron. "Get up, boy," he said, and spoke more harsh words. Melleron jumped as the net that bound him suddenly disappeared.

Wide-eyed, Melleron got stiffly to his feet. Then the magician spoke again, and a single length of the glowing rope appeared in the air. One end hovered as if fastened to something invisible, while the other end looped itself around Melleron's neck.

"Now you can move around," Saelez said with a grin. "You'd best move slowly, though, or you'll be stopped."

Melleron took a wary step, and the cord went with him, drifting weirdly through the air. In the meantime Saelez casually picked up Grit, carried him to the back of the cave, and set him down next to a tiny huddled figure, also in a net.

"Rose!" Melleron cried. He leaped forward, but instantly the cord around his neck jerked him back. Ignoring Saelez's frown, he tried again more slowly, and the trailing cord went with him. Bending over Rose, he saw that her fierce blue eyes were dark with misery – and one loop of the magic net was still wound around her mouth, keeping her silent.

Distress for his friend swept away Melleron's fear. "She can't breathe like that!" he cried,

turning to Saelez. "She can't eat, either! You'll
kill her!"

Saelez glared. "Use a more respectful tone
when you speak to me, slave. The dragon is just
fine – for now."

Before Melleron could reply, Saelez hissed a
word, and the loop of cord that bound Rose's
mouth slid away. She twitched and blinked with
relief, panting.

"If I see one flicker of fire from her," Saelez
snapped, "I'll sew her mouth shut!"

From his cloak he brought out the amazingly thick little book that Melleron had glimpsed before, flicked a page or two, and then spoke a phrase. The nets around Rose and Grit began to expand – instead turning into the bars of small glowing cages, with room for the captives to stand and stretch.

"Is that better, little soft-heart?" Saelez said sarcastically to Melleron. "Now – what do these creatures eat?"

"Rose eats fruit," Melleron said flatly, "and Grit eats stone."

Saelez cackled again. "At least he'll be easy to cater for."

He turned back to the book, then said a few more words. An earthenware bowl full of marsh-plums and silverberries appeared on the table at the center of the cave.

"You feed them," Saelez said airily. "I have work to do."

Moving carefully because of the cord holding him, Melleron gathered up the bowl and went back to the two prisoners.

"Thank you, Melleron," Rose whispered between bites of fruit. "I thought I'd choke in that net – or starve."

"You'll feel better now," Melleron murmured. "I'll get a stone for Grit."

Suddenly, Melleron was dragged sprawling backward by a painful jerk on the magic cord around his neck.

"What are you muttering about?" Saelez snarled, glaring.

"Nothing," Rose said quickly. "We're just trying to keep our spirits up."

Saelez sneered. "Are you dispirited? Too bad, but your woes will end soon, little dragon, when I put an end to you!"

"What do you mean?" Melleron demanded anxiously, getting to his feet.

"You will wish you hadn't asked," the magician snarled. "First, I plan to cast a spell that will make the stone dog love me, as a dog loves its master. Then he will be my loyal, devoted pet and watchdog, my fierce little protector..." He snickered evilly. "After that, I'll work even a more powerful magic – which will make me invulnerable, so no attack, no weapon, can harm me. That spell needs two special ingredients. The skin, and the fresh blood, of a dragon."

"No!" Melleron cried, horrified. "You can't!"

"I can," Saelez snapped, "and I will."

At that moment, Horrimal stirred with a hoarse growl. "Am I to get no rest?" he rumbled. "What is all the shouting?"

"I was informing our guests," Saelez hissed, "what is in store for the small ones."

Horrimal lurched to his feet, looking eager. "Are you ready to do it now?"

"No." The magician's mouth twisted. "The spells are still not... available."

Horrimal scowled. "How long must I wait?"

"I have no idea," Saelez said with a shrug, "but it will be worth waiting for." He stared away, dreamily. "Afterward, we will return to the human lands, where you can continue your private war against the people while I build my palace and begin my new life – an invulnerable lord, whose bidding must be obeyed..."

Horrimal yawned hugely. "I know all that. I just want to watch you do those spells on the little pests. Right now I am weary of this cave. I will go out to sleep in the sun. Later, I think I will go north to my homeland, after all. To bring my friends to join me, in what you call my 'private war'."

Saelez looked disapproving. "Have you forgotten that when you were last in the land of the monsters, your chief put you in chains? Do you remember that I had to rescue you?"

"I can stay clear of the chief and his followers," Horrimal rumbled. "I will be back soon. Open the cave."

"Very well," Saelez muttered, "but keep that magic stone around your neck so I can speak to you." Then he snapped a sharp word, and the cave opened.

Staring out longingly at the sunlight, Melleron felt a small surge of hope as the monster tramped away. We're still trapped, he thought, but one enemy is better than two. All we need now is some sort of chance...

CHAPTER 7

Passing Time

Some days later, far to the south of the cave, Melleron's grandmother was in the village near her cottage, sitting with tears in her eyes in the home of a kindly, gray-haired man – Judge Aldin, leader of the village council.

"Melleron could still be in the forest, maybe hurt or something," she was saying, "but I've looked and looked. I just keep thinking about that monster, and Saelez..." She choked back a sob. "Remember, Saelez was driven out of these lands because he stole children! What if he's stolen my boy?"

Aldin sighed. "It's a terrible thought."

"Can't you help me, Judge Aldin?" Nan pleaded, "you and some of the village men?"

"I'm sorry," the judge said gently. "Finding a lost boy in the mountains would be nearly impossible. Finding a magician who wants to stay hidden would certainly be so. Frankly, not many people would want to go that close to the land of the monsters."

"Then what am I to do?" Nan sobbed desperately.

Aldin patted her hand. "I'm sorry. I know how terribly hard it is to lose a loved one..."

A day or two later, in a wild valley far to the north, two very different beings were talking. They were chatting comfortably, as friends do, although neither of them was human.

One was slim and sleek, covered in brown fur, like a big upright cat – but a cat with huge smooth wings, folded gracefully. She was sitting in the huge marble-elm tree where she lived, in a large nest formed out of its woven branches.

She was talking with a neighbor, who lived in some nearby woods. This was suitable, since he looked like a thorn tree – with a tall thin body and skinny arms and legs, covered in greenish skin like bark and long sharp spikes.

"Are you sure you saw Horrimal, Orani?" the thorny one was asking in a thin sharp voice. "I'm surprised he'd dare to come back."

"It was definitely Horrimal," the winged one said. "He was large as life and twice as ugly. He's a long way from here – down near our southern borders."

The thorny one shook his head, coarse hair rattling like twigs. "What's he up to now? The chief will be livid."

"The chief's always livid about something, Poljon." The winged one laughed, a purring growl. "I don't really think the chief would be likely to start a search down there, although things might get exciting if Horrimal comes back here."

"That would suit me," the thorny one said. "Horrimal might be just what we need to keep from having a boring summer..."

For Melleron, those first days of captivity had been surprisingly quiet. It seemed that a magician's slave had really very little to do. All of the chores and domestic work were easily managed by Saelez's magic. Even their food – a variety of delicacies, for which Melleron had little appetite – simply appeared on the table.

Melleron spent much of his time in idleness, feeling a mixture of boredom and dread. At least he was still allowed to feed Rose and Grit in their cages, and they both remained undaunted, which lifted his spirits.

Also, Saelez still seemed unable to carry out his horrible plan for his small captives. Trying to sound mysterious, he had told Horrimal that the spells weren't "available" – and somehow they still weren't. This made Melleron deeply happy.

Besides, he told himself, idleness was better than being overworked. Therefore, Melleron stayed quiet, trying not to be noticed, while Saelez spent much of his time poring endlessly over his strange thick book, scribbling and mumbling. In fact, Saelez praised Melleron once or twice for being "untroublesome."

This, perhaps, was what led Saelez, one day, to decide that he disliked the magic rope that was still looped around Melleron's neck. "You look like a donkey wearing a halter," the magician cackled. Then, after a quick look into his book, he said two weird words, and the rope vanished.

Then, as Melleron rubbed his neck with relief, Saelez smirked. "We might enjoy some fresh air as well," he said, and spoke another word.

The front of the cave opened wide.

CHAPTER 8

Obedience

Melleron could hardly believe his eyes. It was a dull day outside, with drizzly rain, but it looked wonderful. Saelez turned carelessly away, leaving him by the open cave-mouth. There was nothing at all holding him back.

Heart pounding, Melleron poised himself for an all-out, break-neck sprint toward freedom, but he didn't move.

For one thing, he couldn't run off and desert Rose and Grit. He also saw that while Saelez was moving away as if unconcerned, his head was slightly turned. He's watching me, Melleron realized. He expects me to run. His magic would stop me after the first step.

So – even though every bit of his being was screaming with the urge to run – he let his head droop, and turned to follow Saelez.

The magician looked startled. "You surprise me," he said, smiling. "I was sure you'd run, although that would have proved both pointless and painful for you. Perhaps you've realized you're better off here with me. Well done, Melleron."

The praise made Melleron feel even more miserable. He could hardly look at Rose and Grit later, when he fed them. He was amazed when Rose praised him too.

"You did exactly right, Melleron," she announced through a mouthful of berries. "It's very clever to make him think well of you."

"Is it?" Melleron asked, surprised.

"Very," she told him. "He is growing more at ease with you, less watchful. He has already taken off that cord, giving you free run of the cave. If he gets more off-guard, you might have a chance to get away...!"

"From his magic?" Melleron sighed. "I don't think that's very likely."

Rose's eyes flashed. "There are always chances, Melleron, and there is always hope. For all his power, Saelez is still human, and humans have weaknesses. Watch him – and if you see a chance, take it! If you could get away, you could bring help for us…"

"Rrrr," Grit said encouragingly.

"I don't know where I'd find help," Melleron said dismally. "Anyway, I still can't imagine how I'd escape Saelez's magic, or if I'd have the nerve to try…"

"You were brave and quick and clever before," Rose said firmly, "when we defeated Horrimal. You must be again. Keep making Saelez pleased with you, and stay alert, and never, never, give up hope!"

Over the following day or so Melleron took those words to heart, and did as she said. As Saelez grew more pleased with him, he finally realized why the magician really wanted a slave.

It wasn't to be a servant or a victim, but to be someone to talk to whenever he wished. Most especially, it was to make sure he had someone around to show off to.

During that first evening after Melleron's halter had been removed, Saelez had spent time as usual poring over his strange book, muttering to himself. Then he grew friendly and chatty over supper – talking about the food, the exotic dishes he might magically provide. Melleron made himself listen politely and murmur "yes, sir" now and then.

At last Saelez paused, smiling thinly. "Are you truly interested in the working of magic, Melleron?"

"Yes, sir, I am," Melleron replied, which was true. Melleron found magic itself fascinating. It was Saelez's use of it that was wrong.

The magician nodded. "I should show you more. You've only seen simple bits and pieces and a few upsetting spells, earlier…"

As he thought about those "upsetting" spells, such as the capture of Rose and Grit, a shadow darkened Melleron's eyes. Saelez saw it, but he misunderstood.

"You mustn't be afraid," he smiled. He leaned closer. "Why – I might even let you cast a spell yourself!"

"Me?" Melleron cried, astonished.

"Certainly," Saelez smirked. "Of course, for any major spells you would need some natural ability, along with years of study and special preparation. Anyone can perform a simple spell, however – with this."

Then, even more astonishingly, he brought out the mysterious book from his cloak, and casually handed it to Melleron.

Melleron almost dropped it, for it was not only incredibly thick but unexpectedly heavy, and covered in shiny leather that felt cold and slippery. Opening it carefully, he blinked at the dark writing that crowded the pages, too impossibly tiny to read.

When his fingers touched a page, it suddenly and shockingly enlarged, so that every word was clear.

Then Saelez reached over and took the book away. "It's a spell-book, made by a group of master-wizards. I... acquired it from my own teacher, just before he died. It contains thousands and thousands of spells, large and small..." He turned a few pages, then handed the book back to Melleron. "There, at the top of the left-hand page, is a nice easy spell. It's only one word. Try it."

The word was strange and hard to say, but on his second try Melleron got it right. He nearly fell off his chair – for on the table before him appeared a small but perfect cake, glazed with melted sugar.

Saelez cackled merrily at the look on his face. "Well done! Now you too are a magician! You may eat the cake – it's quite real..."

Warily Melleron took a bite, but it seemed perfectly normal and delicious. As he ate, he was staring at the spell-book. What if I could find a spell, he thought excitedly, that would help Rose and Grit and me escape... ?

CHAPTER 9

Pages of Magic

"What are you thinking?" Saelez asked, reaching for the book again. "That you'd like to turn yourself into a whistle-fly and buzz away?"

"Oh, no, sir," Melleron said, trying to look innocent.

"Anyway, you couldn't," Saelez told him. "To be a shape-changer, a magician must undergo many rigorous, dangerous rituals, over a long time. Only then will the spells work when he speaks them." He smirked. "Not every student of magic can face that preparation, but I did – and I am now a master of shape-changing."

He had been turning pages in his book as he spoke. Glancing down with a twisted grin, he spoke a rasping sentence. Then he was gone and in his place sat a giant slavering howler-bear.

Surprise as much as fright made Melleron fling himself back with a cry, almost overturning his chair. The bear became Saelez again, laughing gleefully.

"You're a fearful little one, aren't you?" he cackled. "Did you think you were about to be eaten?" He laughed and laughed, as Melleron tried to smile.

Over the next day or so, it became Saelez's favorite entertainment – sudden shape-changes to frighten Melleron. At any moment Melleron might find himself face to face with a snarling blood-wolf, an oversized spider-bat, a grinning skeleton, or even a huge and fur-covered tusked rock lion.

Each time he followed Rose's advice about playing up to Saelez, and pretended to be terrified, as the magician seemed to enjoy his fear so much.

Meanwhile, he carefully watched Saelez's every move whenever he brought out his spell-book. If we're ever to have a chance, he kept thinking, it might come from the book. Rose agreed – though neither she nor Melleron could figure out how to get past the fact that Saelez always kept the book safe.

"Never mind," Rose told him. "Thanks to you, we have much more hope now than we had before. Keep on as you are, Melleron, and something will turn up."

So Melleron went on being a humble slave and a good audience, biding his time, and learning more about the spell-book.

"The book has its own peculiar magic," Saelez told him when they were sitting at the table one evening. "Look at how its pages enlarge, for instance. It's also indestructible – it can't be torn up or burned or anything. Even stranger, although there are thousands of spells in it, as I told you, they aren't always the same spells!"

Spells constantly vanished from the book, he explained, and were replaced by others that had vanished before, perhaps long before, and were making a reappearance. No one ever knew when a spell might vanish, or when it might come back to the pages of the book.

"That's why I'm still waiting," Saelez grumbled, "to deal with your little friends." He scowled at the spell-book, and set it on the table. "The spells that I plan to use on them have vanished from the book, and haven't yet reappeared."

Good, Melleron thought. "Why does the book do that, sir?" he asked.

"The wizards who made the book probably found it amusing," Saelez sniffed. "I guess it is also because with this design, the book can contain an enormous number of spells and still be small enough to carry around. All in all, there are more than a million spells in it – but only a few thousand are actually there at any one time, do you see? It's frankly thick and heavy enough just with those."

"Couldn't you have more than one book?" Melleron asked carefully.

Saelez shook his head gloomily. "The magic won't allow copies of any sort. I do keep writing out important spells, and also trying to commit them to memory, in case they disappear from the book, but it's no good. Written copies last awhile – often for days – but then, without fail, they start to fade, and soon vanish." He sighed. "Copies of copies fade even more quickly. Spells in the memory linger for only a few hours before they are forgotten…"

Melleron's eyes widened as the realization struck him. If Saelez lost the book, before long he would lose all his magical power! If only, he thought. If only…

"Still," the magician said, as if echoing his thought, "as long as the book is close at hand, I can refresh my memory of certain spells whenever I want." He smiled nastily.

The smile was just enough warning. Snarling an ugly phrase, Saelez abruptly changed himself into an oversized, hissing fen-lizard. Melleron shrieked and cowered in pretended terror, crumpling his face as if about to burst into tears.

Saelez reappeared, laughing delightedly. "Poor little faint-heart – am I being unkind? Don't cry. I'll become something nice for you. Something harmless and pretty…"

Flicking through the spell-book, he spoke another few words, and changed again into a broad-winged, brilliantly colored paint-box butterfly. The gorgeous creature fluttered over the table, as if showing off its colors…

Without thought or hesitation, Melleron snatched up a heavy soup ladle and smashed the butterfly out of the air.

CHAPTER 10

Running North

As the insect dropped limply toward the floor, it turned back into Saelez, landing with a crash, unconscious and sprawled, breathing raggedly. Melleron whirled, snatched up the spell-book and sprang to Rose and Grit.

"What happened?" Rose cried – they couldn't see from the back of the cave.

Melleron explained in a rush, frantically turning the pages of the book, looking for a spell that would release them. He desperately hoped to find the one that Saelez had used to remove the cord from his neck.

Although he couldn't remember that spell itself, he did remember that it was quite near the front of the book...

"We need the magic that opens the cave too," Rose said anxiously.

"Yes, I know," Melleron gasped. Then he stopped, stiffening. "There it is!" he muttered tensely. "Now..."

He took a deep breath, then spoke two long words that were a series of harsh sounds.

Nothing happened.

"Hang on," Melleron muttered. "I think I said it wrong..." He spoke the words again, with a different tone in the last syllable.

Instantly, the glowing cages vanished, as if they had never been.

All three of them cried out in relief and triumph. As they fled across the cave, they paused to inspect Saelez – still sprawled and unconscious.

"Rrr, rrr," Grit growled fiercely.

"Grit says it's too bad he's not still a butterfly," Rose said. "Then we could squash him and finish him off for good."

Melleron looked faintly sick. "I really don't think I could do that."

"No," Rose agreed. "We can't hurt him as he is. It would be too bloodthirsty."

"Let's just get away from here," Melleron said. Going back to the book, turning a few more pages, he found the single magic word he needed. Carefully, he spoke it.

The cave-mouth opened, revealing a soft summer twilight, with a gentle breeze.

"You're getting good at magic, Melleron," Rose laughed as they raced away down the slope and across the meadow.

"It's the spell-book, not me," Melleron said, cramming the book in his shirt as he ran.

"It's your magic if you're doing it," Rose pointed out. "Anyway, won't Saelez lose his power, now that he doesn't have the book?"

"Not right away," Melleron said. "No one can remember spells for long, but he has copies of a lot of spells. He said that written copies don't fade away for a few days."

"Rrrrr," Grit said.

"Right," Rose agreed. "That means if he isn't badly hurt, he could still turn into a hawk or something, and come after us. We'd better keep going without stopping tonight, to get as far away as we can before sunrise."

Melleron frowned. "There's Horrimal to think about too. He and Saelez are both likely to chase us, all the way back to the Peaceful Forest."

"Rrr," Grit growled.

"Yes," Rose said quietly. "That's why we're not going back there."

By then they were moving up a gravelly slope. Melleron stopped, staring at Rose through the twilight. "Not going... ?"

"Not yet," Rose said. "We can't just keep running. We have to find a way to get free of Saelez and Horrimal for good. For that we are going to need help."

"Who can help us?" Melleron asked weakly.

"Our chief, and our friends, who'd be able to handle Horrimal and possibly Saelez too, if they wanted to," Rose said. "We have to go north, Melleron, to the land of the monsters."

As they hurried on along a high ridge, Melleron fell silent, thinking uneasily about the fearful land they were heading toward. Rose always said that many of its monsters were friendly – but he kept thinking about the others...

Also, he was silent to save breath. Grit's stony strength was tireless, but Rose's slim wings soon grew weary, and Melleron was worn out by the evening's dramas. Still, they dared not stop, even when the ridge led to a series of rugged slopes, with treacherous drops half-hidden in the moonlight. As the hours passed, Melleron became more and more exhausted, stumbling blindly along behind Grit.

He nearly fell on his face when the little dog suddenly stopped with a growl – while Rose hissed softly and drifted higher into the air.

Blinking, Melleron saw the glassy-gray light of dawn in the east. They were standing on an easy slope that was taking them down, into a leafy vale.

Of course Horrimal had brought them through the worst of the mountains, to the cave. Now, Melleron realized, they had come most of the rest of the way – down from the cruel cliffs and ridges, onto the gentler, greener northern foothills.

Why had they stopped? Then, through his weariness, Melleron heard what his friends had heard. There were rough, harsh, growling voices, not far away.

"Monsters," Rose said, swirling down. "I'll go and look."

As she soared away, the growling voices seemed to draw nearer – then suddenly became a burst of loud roaring, making Melleron jump. Had Rose been seen? He could also hear heavy crashing and crackling in the brush... Those sounds quickly began to fade, as if the monsters were rushing off the other way.

After a time that seemed to last forever, Melleron jumped again when Grit growled. Then he started wagging his stubby tail as Rose came swooping down onto a bush.

"It was Horrimal," she said breathlessly, "with that gang of his – headed south. I think they spotted me... One of them must have very good eyes..."

"Saelez must be all right, then," Melleron said gloomily. "He must have called Horrimal back with that magic stone."

"Horrimal could be going south for his own reasons," Rose pointed out. "Anyway, I led them in the wrong direction for a way, then I lost them. We'll be safe enough if we keep going for a while."

Nearly an hour later, when Rose was sure that they had left the gang of monsters far behind, she had another idea.

"What about magic, Melleron?" she asked. "Do you think you could find a spell in that book to hide us?"

"I can look," Melleron mumbled wearily, "but there are thousands of spells in the book – it could take ages..."

"Never mind, then," Rose said, yawning daintily. "We'll hide ourselves. No one's after us now, and I'm tired."

They found a cozy thicket and slept, well hidden and undisturbed. The next day they kept moving north. As they went along, Melleron tried looking through the book to find a spell that would hide them. He found nothing, and soon gave up after he nearly walked into a tree two different times.

Still, Rose kept careful watch from the air. She saw no signs of pursuit, but improved their situation by spotting a butter-apple tree with some early fruit. Rested and fed – there were plenty of pebbles for Grit – they covered a good deal of ground that day. In the evening they decided against pushing on through the dark.

"We're in the clear," Rose said, smiling. "We don't have to wear ourselves out. Tomorrow, we'll be in the land of the monsters."

That made Melleron shiver a little, but by sunrise they were mostly concerned about being hungry as they set off again. Before long they entered a broad valley, like a giant basin with low hills around it. Rose swirled around them in a joyous circle.

"We've crossed the border!" she cried. "We're home, we're safe, and we can have breakfast!" She pointed with a wing. "Over there, not far, is a silverberry grove!" She waved the other wing. "Over on that hill is a stony patch, with plenty of flints…"

With that Grit went bounding hungrily away. Rose sighed, then laughed. "You find the berries, Melleron," she said. "I'll try to keep Grit from eating the hillside…"

She swooped away, while Melleron trotted eagerly in the direction she had shown. In that quiet green-clad valley, with the prospect of silverberries making his mouth water, he forgot all his earlier uneasiness. In a few moments he was devouring the big juicy berries just as if he were in his own forest.

Then he heard the scream.

It was a faraway cry, shrill and wild, but he knew it was Rose's voice. It froze him rigid, with a berry halfway to his mouth. Then he jerked, dropping the berry, hearing slightly fainter sounds, fierce and rough, like some he had heard not long before.

It was the growling and roaring of monsters.

CHAPTER 11

Alone

The terror that gripped him suddenly released him, like a bowstring releasing an arrow. In a headlong sprint he raced toward the sounds, in the direction that Rose and Grit had taken. He was still running at full speed, white-faced and wild-eyed, when he reached a place where the side of a low hill showed a deep cleft, bright with flinty stone.

It was silent, deserted – but he knew it was where Grit and Rose had been, where the terrible sounds had come from. He didn't need a forester's skills to read the clear and dreadful signs. Torn-up turf, broken bushes, scarred earth with marks of huge clawed feet, and possibly a splash of blood...

Rose and Grit had been attacked by monsters, and had lost the unequal battle.

Dazed by horror, Melleron roamed the area, looking for some sign of hope. He was crouched by another blood-smear, desperately hoping it wasn't from Rose, when he glimpsed a movement on top of the low hill.

With fright flaring through him he dropped behind a low bush, peered up through the leaves, and saw a monstrosity. A tall, upright, bulky creature with lumpy purple skin, red eyes, and a blunt muzzle filled with jagged teeth.

The monster half-turned, glancing back. "Thought I saw something," he growled.

Five other frightful creatures loomed up onto the hilltop, staring down.

One of them had thick plates of gray hide like armor, and growths like daggers along his spine. The second was squat and hairless, with dead-white skin, extra-long teeth, and a spiny ruff. The third was small and scaly with hooked claws and bulging eyes. The fourth was as huge and shaggy as Horrimal, but without horns and with thick brown hair, not black.

The fifth monster in the group was Horrimal himself.

"What was it?" he rumbled.

"Something was moving over there," the tall purple one said.

"The boy!" Horrimal growled. "I knew he would be nearby..."

The armored one grunted. "Any human youngster would run like crazy the other way, if he heard the noise we were making."

"Not this one," Horrimal growled. "Come and look around."

The five of them started down the hillside.

Every bit of Melleron wanted to scream and run. Instead, calling on his forest instincts, he slid silently away through the tall grass, slipping from bush to bush.

Behind him he could hear the monsters growling as they searched around where he had been seen. When he looked back from behind a small goldfir, he saw the six of them moving in his direction.

They also seemed to be arguing – and Horrimal had the last word. "It will not hurt us to keep looking for the boy," he growled, his words clear to Melleron. "Saelez will reward us, if we find him..."

Melleron nearly collapsed in fresh panic. So Saelez was unhurt, and Horrimal and the others must have met him in the mountains, and received instructions to begin their pursuit.

Saelez might also be somewhere close by, vengefully searching...

Behind him, the six horrors had fanned out, tramping forward in a widespread line, searching a broad sweep of land. If he moved sideways, to try to slip past them, he might be spotted. He couldn't hide and hope to stay unseen as they went past. He had to stay ahead of them. This meant he was heading north.

He didn't want to go that way. Rose had hoped to get help from the chief of the monsters, but Melleron doubted whether the chief would help him. Even if he knew where to find the chief, or had the nerve to ask.

Yet he had no choice. He was being driven northward.

Shivering, terrified, desperately alone, he crept away like a hunted animal, deeper into the heart of that inhuman land.

The strange slow hunt went on through the day, farther and farther across the valley.

The spread-out line of the monsters advanced steadily, peering under every shrub, watching all around. Melleron kept on creeping behind bushes, slithering through grass; he was unable to hurry, so fearful was he of making a twig snap or a branch thrash.

Even so, by mid-afternoon he had drawn well ahead of them. He relaxed a little, worn down by tension and weariness, and then he made a slip – stumbling against a lady-birch sapling, which bent and flailed.

Behind him he heard a faint shrill cry. "There! There he is!"

Crouching, staring back, Melleron saw the monsters, looking small at that distance, beside a lofty orchid-tree. There was another smaller shape high in the treetop, which he realized was the scaly monster with the bulging eyes – sharp, long-sighted eyes that had spotted the sapling's movement.

At once the monsters charged forward, the scaly one whisking down the tree and following.

Melleron scrambled away, his weariness forgotten, straining not to make any more giveaway mistakes. Somehow he kept his distance ahead of them.

Fresh panic was gathering in him. He was managing to hide from them and stay ahead of them, but they were far stronger, and would be able to keep coming all day and all night. What if some of them could see like cats in the dark? What if he made more mistakes, as he grew more tired?

He needed to get clear of them, to find a hideaway where he could rest, and the valley's scattered brush and long grass would not provide it.

Then, as the afternoon wore on, he snaked through the grass to the top of a low rise, and saw a broad dark band like a wall, in the distance ahead. This nearly made him whoop with joy.

It was a forest, or at least a big expanse of woods, looking wonderfully thick and dense. He could hide from hundreds of monsters in there!

He crept on, smiling slightly. While he was safely hidden in the trees, he thought, he could go on looking for a special way not only to hide but to escape. A magic way, using the spell-book.

CHAPTER 12

Magical Mist

At about the same time, far to the south, a lonely figure was plodding along a path in the Peaceful Forest. Melleron's grandmother, weary and drawn, was spending another day in the forest, as she did every day. Searching.

She had found no sign of Melleron, in any of the forest's secret ways and places. She knew it was most likely that Melleron had been carried off, to the mountains or beyond. Yet she kept on, searching the forest.

She did so because she clung to a tiny hope that he might be there.

With Melleron gone, she couldn't simply sit in her cottage and do nothing. She would go on searching, the next day, and the next... As long as she was able...

Meanwhile, far to the north, the strange being like a thorn tree was standing among spiky bushes, picking bristle-pears, when his catlike winged friend settled gracefully on the turf beside him.

"Orani, my friend!" he said brightly. "What's the latest gossip?"

The winged one smiled at him and stretched her wings gracefully. "You'll like this, Poljon. You know those five boneheads who always hung around with Horrimal? They've gone off to join him."

"So Horrimal's recruiting," the thorny one said thoughtfully. "He must be planning something interesting..."

"You never know," the winged one said. "Anyway, the chief's in a temper again."

"Is he going to do anything about it?" the thorny one asked.

"He's talking about going south for a look," the winged one said. "It may just be talk. Still, I might fly back down there and sniff around a little bit to see what's really going on."

"Mm," the thorny one said. "I might go myself. The Greenwood there is lovely." He grinned. "Anyway, why should we let Horrimal have all the fun?"

Also about the same time, back in the valley where Melleron was being hunted, a fierce-eyed swallow-hawk swooped down into a sheltered clearing. Horrimal and his friends were there, lolling in the late-afternoon sun, with scraps of food scattered on the turf, and a large cloth sack lying on one side.

The hawk landed, shimmered, and became the cloaked figure of Saelez – with a strip of cloth around his head like a bandage, his eyes glittering furiously.

"Well?" he snapped at Horrimal. "When we spoke through the magic stone, you said you had found the boy! Where is he?"

Horrimal waved a huge hand. "He's up ahead somewhere. Not far."

"Then why are you lying around here?" Saelez almost shrieked.

"We're resting," Horrimal rumbled. "We have been searching all day."

"The boy's got to be worn out too, by now," the purple monster added.

Saelez snorted. "The boy is very capable in the wilds, as you should know by now. He could be getting even farther ahead!"

"Then go look for him," said the bulging-eyed one, snickering.

"I intend to," Saelez fumed. "I expect the rest of you to do the same. Before nightfall, I want him in my hands!"

Shortly afterward, Melleron entered the woodland, which was every bit as dense and overgrown as he had hoped. Knowing that the monsters had fallen farther behind, he went a little deeper, then paused to look through the spell-book, still hoping to find a simple spell, easily managed, that would hide him magically.

With all the thousands of spells in the bulky little book, he spent a long, edgy time flicking through the pages, finding nothing of use. Growing nervous, after having glanced through nearly half of the book, he was getting ready to give up. After turning a few more pages, he saw a spell with a few short lines. It was a magic recipe for a Cloud of Safekeeping.

Reading it swiftly, he saw that the spell needed simply a selection of herbs, fresh water to moisten them, a plain pattern drawn on the ground, and a few words. No more. Almost laughing out loud, he went to work.

The herbs were common ones, growing all around. When he had gathered enough, he found a brook nearby and moistened them as required. Then, in a hollow beneath some leafy trees, he drew a long oval shape on the ground and scattered the wet leaves around its edge. Finally, he stepped into the oval, peering at the book through the dimness – as the afternoon waned toward sunset – and read out the words.

At once the wet leaves began to steam gently. As the steam rose, it thickened into a mist. The Cloud of Safekeeping gathered around him like a veil.

It looks just like any other patch of mist, he thought, that might form in a shaded hollow. Taking a chance, he stepped out of the oval – but the mist stayed still, looking as perfectly ordinary as he hoped. Also, while he had been able to see dimly through it from inside, it seemed thicker from the outside, so that everything within the oval was entirely hidden.

Sighing with relief and weariness, Melleron crept back into the mist, pulling leaves together for a bed, while sunset drew an extra veil of darkness around him.

CHAPTER 13

Terror in the Woods

It seemed only a moment before birdsong woke him into a sunlit morning. The mist-cloud around him looked a little ragged, as if it might not last much longer, but all else was peaceful. Moving away, he crept back to the edge of the woods and gazed across the valley.

Clearly the pursuing monsters had also stopped for the night, for their dark shapes were still quite distant. But they were still hunting... still advancing...

Good, he thought, drawing back into the greenery. They were definitely heading toward the woods, and should arrive before long. When they had arrived, he could start circling safely through the dense cover, doubling back past them, and be away – to the south – before they knew he'd turned.

Then, somehow, he would try to find out what had happened to his friends.

Drifting back into the deep woods, he found a patch of wild sweetbeans and had breakfast, feeling almost at ease. He felt completely at home in the woodland, he was far less exposed there, and now he had his magic mist to protect him as well.

But did he? Suddenly chilled, he remembered that spells could vanish from the spell-book, without warning... Snatching the book from inside his shirt, he saw with relief that the mist-spell hadn't vanished. Still, it might, any time, and he needed it – especially to get himself back across the valley.

The anxiety stayed with him through the morning as he waited for the monsters to reach the woods. At midday, he was crouching in a cluster of lady-birch trees, still waiting – when the sight of the birches' loose peeling bark jogged his memory.

He thought about Saelez, in the cave, endlessly copying out important spells.

Quickly pulling away a length of birch-bark, he found a sharp-pointed twig, and wrote out the mist-spell – scratching the letters deeply into the soft smooth bark.

He knew from Saelez that copied-out spells faded away, in time, though not as soon as remembered ones. While he could write it out again, whenever it started to fade from the bark, he also knew that copies of copies faded even more rapidly.

Still, having the copy made him feel better. If the precious spell did vanish from the book, the copy might last long enough to get him across the valley.

On impulse, because there was room on the bark, he also copied out the two other small spells that he had used before – the brief spell that had removed the glowing ropes, and the single word that had conjured the little cake. He even tried that one again, and the cake that appeared was just as tasty as the first one.

When he was done, he rolled up the piece of bark and slid it down into his sock, so it wouldn't be lost or crumpled. Then he moved off for a drink at a small clear spring that he had spotted earlier. Clumps of bread-root plants grew by the spring, and he was happily digging some up – when he heard a voice.

It was a monstrous voice, frighteningly near. It wasn't Horrimal's rumble, but was a weirdly hollow and booming voice.

"I really hate all this trudging around," the voice was saying. "When we find that wretch, wherever he is, I'm going to make him suffer."

Melleron slid noiselessly aside, into a low trench hidden in tangleweed, just in time.

Seven frightful monsters – which he had never seen before – were marching toward the spring, toward him.

He saw a shaggy one and a scaly one, a bulky one and a bony one, a dark one who looked like an insect, and a pale one who looked like a fungus. The one that scared him the most was the one in the center, who had the loud booming voice. This monster was immense, twice as tall as any of the others, with four huge arms – along with long thick trailing yellow hair, and giant dagger-sharp tusks.

Melleron flattened himself, wriggling deeper into the weeds, at the sound of a new voice – from above. A catlike monster with wide smooth wings circled down to land among them.

"I haven't seen a thing," the winged one announced, "but it's not easy to search woodland from the air."

"Believe me, it's no easier searching down here," the four-armed giant grumbled. "Do you think he has left the woods? We could be wasting our time…"

"I would have seen him, out in more open country," the winged one said. "No, he's in here somewhere. We'll find him."

"Soon, I hope," the giant one boomed. "Because I'm getting really annoyed. I'm beginning to think I might just rip off his head."

In that moment, as Melleron huddled in the weeds trying not to tremble, another flash of terror clutched at him. A short distance away, he saw a bird move slightly on a branch. The bird seemed to be hiding among the leaves, watching the monsters.

It was a swallow-hawk.

CHAPTER 14

Circling Away

The hawk's yellow eyes held an unnatural glitter, and a swallow-hawk was Saelez's favorite shape for traveling...

Melleron stared at it, frozen, as a trapped hareling looks at a real hawk. Then the monsters tramped off, and were soon out of sight among the trees. The hawk in turn spread its wings and flew away. Before long Melleron crept out of the weeds and fled as well.

He kept an extra-careful watch as he went along, for he had no doubt that he was the one the new monsters were seeking. Who else was being hunted in those woods? Those horrors had to be more of Horrimal's gang.

Still, even though he moved around all morning – stealthily, quiveringly alert – he had no further glimpses of groups of monsters or of swallow-hawks. Pausing for a rest at midday, he played it safe by summoning his mist again. He was pleased to find the spell still unchanged in the book, and also still clear on the roll of bark hidden in his sock.

Safely hidden, paging idly through the book while nibbling some of the bread-roots that he had dug up before, he noticed a spell on the very last page – one that hadn't been there before. Clearly it was a spell that had disappeared from the book previously, and had just reappeared, as spells did. It was a shock – because it showed how to destroy the spell-book.

So the book wasn't indestructible, as Saelez had claimed. If it were destroyed, Saelez would lose his power once his copies faded away, as they were sure to do.

Well, it can't happen yet, Melleron decided grimly – not while he still needed the book.

He was surprised to find that he felt slightly sad about the idea of destroying it at all. It was so exciting and amazing to do even the small spells he could manage. Then there was the added pleasure of using Saelez's own magic book to escape from him and his allies...

If I kept the book, he said dreamily to himself, I could try to learn how to do bigger spells. I could be – Melleron the Magician!

That made him smile, but not for long. He knew that while he had the book, he would never be safe. Saelez would never stop hunting him, because he would never stop wanting the book back for his own use.

So, to stop Saelez, he thought, the book would have to be destroyed. As he read through the spell of destruction he saw that it was hugely difficult – weird and complex, with a long list of unpleasant ingredients. Then he saw something else as he peered more closely.

A few added lines, even tinier, gave a "Swifter Way" to destroy the book.

As he read, Melleron's eyes filled with tears. Once he might have been able to use that

Swifter Way, because it required only one special thing. Unfortunately, that was something that he had lost, and might never find again...

The sadness stayed with him for the rest of the day. So did tension and fear, because during those hours he decided to start his careful circle that would take him out of the woodland, leaving all the crowds of monsters behind. To avoid being seen or leaving any trace, he had to move very slowly, with extra care, through the thickest undergrowth he could find. He did this for many hours, circling away one silent step at a time, hardly disturbing a leaf.

At that pace, he knew, he would still be in the woods when night fell, but the mist-spell was still in the book, reassuring him. Indeed, he stopped just after sunset, weary from hours of concentration, when he came upon a narrow gully to make his mist.

Settling into his hideaway, munching another bread-root, he looked at his copied spells on the birch-bark, and cut a few of the words more deeply where they seemed to have started fading a little. Then, with the last of the daylight fading as well, he tucked the bark back into his sock and settled himself to sleep.

Sunrise found him awake, rested, and ready for another day of stealthy creeping through the thickets, hiding from the monstrous hunters. Carefully he studied the woods all around, but saw only greenery, heard only birds and insects. He stepped out of the mist, and started moving up out of the gully.

Behind him, shattering the stillness, he heard a hiss of astonishment. A sharp, startled voice said, "What's this? A boy?"

He whirled and saw a tree stalking swiftly toward him.

Through his terror, Melleron realized it was a monster who looked like a thorn tree, with a narrow greenish body and spindly, spiky limbs. "Where did you come from, boy?" it demanded, reaching out a thorn-clawed hand.

Melleron hurtled frantically away, as the thorn-monster cried, "No – come back!" He raced on, weaving among trees, leaping through brush, until he could run no more. Gasping for breath, he huddled by a huge tree, quivering.

Nothing seemed to be chasing him – but still he felt unnerved. He had come into an area of unusually tall, straight whitebeech trees, forming a thick canopy overhead. This meant there was almost no undergrowth, save for a few tough weeds and small flowers.

Nowhere to hide or shelter...

A rustle made him leap with new shock. Dropping to the ground at the base of the tree, he slid into a shallow pit among its thick arched roots. Peering past the roots, heart thumping, he waited to see what new menace had arrived.

Suddenly, all he could feel was astonishment. With another rustle of leaves, and a flutter of wings, something small and bright pink swooped down to settle on a patch of moss.

CHAPTER 15

Joy and Horror

"Rose!" In his delight, Melleron might have shrieked the name, but instinct turned it into a strangled whisper.

"There you are, Melleron," the little dragon said brightly. "I've been looking for you everywhere."

"I was going to try to look for you," Melleron babbled, leaping up. "Are you all right? What happened to you? Where's Grit?"

"Grit?" Rose said. "Oh – he's in the woods somewhere, and I'm fine. We were attacked by Horrimal and his gang, but we got away."

"I thought you'd been hurt, or killed," Melleron said breathlessly. "I saw the signs of a fight... and there was blood..."

"Not mine, I'm glad to say," Rose replied, with a sharp laugh. "I've been very worried, Melleron. I had no idea where you might be, with all those monsters after you."

"I came across the valley..." Melleron began. Then he paused, puzzled. "How did you know the monsters were after me, Rose?"

She twitched. "Why, I... I know Horrimal and his friends are here in these woods, so I imagined they came in here after you. I bet it's because you have the spell-book." She peered at him intently. "You do still have it, don't you, Melleron?"

It seemed an odd question for her to ask just then, Melleron thought, especially in such a hungry tone of voice. She seemed unconcerned about Grit... and she was being vague, not like her usual self... and the brightness in her eyes looked different somehow...

Suspicion growing, he had an idea. "Don't worry about the book, Rose," he said. "Worry about yourself. It's not safe here for someone who's bright pink..."

Bracing himself, he waited for the explosion, the stream of raging blue fire. The little dragon merely waved a wing. "Don't worry. I'll be all right..." she began.

Icy fear swept over Melleron, and he took a shaky step back. "You're not Rose!" he gasped, and turned to run.

He wasn't fast enough. The false Rose shimmered and became the hooded figure of Saelez, face twisting with fury as he snapped a harsh word.

As Melleron tried to leap away, a length of the glowing magic rope looped itself around his neck, and dragged him thrashing to the ground.

Saelez's laughter was humorless and bitter. "Did you think you had killed me, my treacherous little slave?" he snarled. "Or did you merely think you left me powerless when you stole my book?"

Melleron said nothing, struggling helplessly against the rope that tethered him.

"Clearly you forgot about my written copies of spells," Saelez went on. Moving threateningly forward, he pulled a sheaf of papers from within his cloak. "These spells have lasted well, so I'm far from powerless." He stuffed the papers away, his eyes flaming. "Now I want my book, boy! I want it immediately!"

Melleron shrank back. As Saelez thrust out a bony hand to grab him, he was halted by the sound of thudding feet. Horrimal and his five followers were arriving at a run.

"Why have you called us to this place, Saelez?" Horrimal growled. "We need to get out of these woods. We have seen signs of other monsters... many of them..."

"I'm sure I saw that Orani flying above the trees!" the bulging-eyed creature cried. "They must be looking for us!"

"Let them look," Saelez sneered, with a careless wave of his hand.

Horrimal's yellow eyes blazed. "You may not care," he rumbled, "but we do!"

In that moment, no one was looking directly at Melleron. Saelez had turned to glare at Horrimal, and it seemed that the monsters hadn't noticed him yet, for the rope around his neck had pulled him back down among the roots of the great tree.

Stealthily, he drew the spell-book from his shirt. For a moment he thought of using it to free himself – but there was no time to search through it for a suitable spell, and Saelez would certainly see it if he tried. So, instead, he pushed it down as carefully as he could into a dark corner of the shallow pit beneath the roots.

CHAPTER 16

Captives Again

"We can't just turn into birds and fly off the way you can!" the tall purple monster was snarling at Saelez.

"We could all end up in chains if they find us!" roared the brown shaggy one.

"They will certainly find you," Saelez snapped, "if you go on making so much noise!" In the sudden silence, he went on. "I simply meant that the others will look in vain, because we'll be gone!" He pointed. "I have the boy!"

Horrimal and the others looked and grinned, growling their approval.

"With my spell-book, I can distract the others," Saelez went on. He turned to glare at Melleron. "So, now, boy – give me the book."

"I don't have it," Melleron said, letting his voice tremble slightly.

The magician's bony hands curved like talons. "What do you mean, you don't have it?" he screeched.

"Not so loud," the bulging-eyed monster whined nervously.

"I threw it away," Melleron said. It was almost a whimper, as he slid back into the weak and timid role he had played in the cave. "In the mountains. I didn't want to carry it. It… it scared me."

Saelez reached out, ablaze with fury. "It is I who should scare you," he rasped.

Gripping Melleron's shirt-front, he searched him, quickly and roughly – pockets, shirt, trouser legs, anywhere that might be able to hide a thick heavy book.

"So it's true," he hissed furiously at last. "The little faint-heart, fearing the book of power, simply threw it away. The most precious object in the world is *gone*!"

"He was not so fearful when he attacked you," Horrimal rumbled.

"That would have been a sudden impulse," Saelez sniffed. "Had he stopped to think, he would have been terrified."

"So do we twist his neck?" the scaly monster asked hopefully.

"Oh, no," Saelez snarled. "We'll take him back to the mountains, so he can show me the exact spot where he threw the book away. If he doesn't, he will suffer, terribly, as will his friends." He beckoned to the squat hairless monster. "Show him."

The hairless one had a large cloth sack slung over his shoulder, which Melleron hadn't noticed. With a grin, the monster dumped its contents on the ground.

It was Rose and Grit, tightly bound once again, and gagged with the glowing cord.

Saelez sneered at Melleron's horrified expression. "They're unharmed," he snarled. "I need them alive for the magic I plan for them." He turned to Horrimal. "Now we must hurry. We have to find the book as soon as possible…"

"We?" Horrimal growled. "Do you expect us to dig around in the mountains trying to find your book for you?"

"Forget it!" the armored monster barked. "We came to go raiding, not chasing around after boys and books!"

Saelez looked outraged. "Fools," he snapped, "don't you realize that book is as vital to you as to me? You need my magic…"

The others growled, Saelez hissed, and in that new outburst of quarreling none of them was looking at Melleron. Only Rose and Grit were watching, in silent desperation.

Giving them a small tense smile, he reached down to his sock – untouched by Saelez's rough search. Drawing out the slim roll of bark, he almost moaned with relief. All the spells were still there. A few letters were slightly faded, but readable.

In a clear, steady voice, he spoke the words that banished the glowing cords.

In the midst of the quarrel Saelez heard him, and spun wildly around. He was just in time to see Rose and Grit, freed from their bonds, hurl themselves into battle.

Shrieking, Rose flew at Saelez like a small pink missile. She was in such a fury that her flame ignited, blasting blue fire at the magician's face.

Howling, Saelez leaped back, tripped, and tumbled into a straggling patch of hookweed.

In the same instant Grit leaped at Horrimal, his growl almost a roar, and sank his diamond teeth into a shaggy ankle. Horrimal bellowed and kicked, shaking Grit off, but the little dog simply lunged at one of the others.

Suddenly, all six monsters were in a frantic roaring muddle, stumbling and lurching, crashing into each other, trying to grab Grit or kick him while dodging his teeth, more often grabbing or kicking one another...

Saelez was screeching and flailing, trying to free his cloak from the barbs of the hookweed, cowering away from Rose's flame and her swooping raging attacks...

Then Melleron dived down into the pit among the roots, snatched up the spell-book, thrust it and the roll of bark into his shirt, and screamed over all the noise.

"Rose! Grit! Come on!"

CHAPTER 17

Surrounded

He leaped away, again weaving among the trees at breakneck speed. Rose and Grit abandoned their battles and joined him, flashing through the woods with the bellowing monsters thundering in pursuit.

The three friends, far swifter, gained ground on their pursuers, so the bellowing grew more distant. At the same time, the open area among the whitebeeches was giving way to denser, more tangled bush. As they plunged in among the screening brush, Melleron glanced quickly back – and felt a new cold stab of fear.

Some distance behind, a swallow-hawk was swooping among the trees.

Then Melleron stopped and looked again. There was something wrong with the hawk. It was flying erratically, diving, swerving, flapping… Its wings didn't look right, and its tail was mostly missing…

"Look," Melleron whispered to his friends, who had stopped with him. "It's Saelez. His shape-changing magic has gone wrong. The copied spells he's using must be fading."

"Rrrr," Grit growled.

"He says we can escape Saelez and the monsters in these thickets," Rose said.

Melleron nodded. "We'll swing away to the left, then start making our way out of the woods altogether." He grinned. "Wait till I show you my mist-cloud!"

They raced on through the tangled, shadowed undergrowth, twisting and ducking as they fought their way through it as quickly and quietly as they could. A moment later the thick brush came to a startling end, so that they almost fell out of it into a bright open area, where only grass and flowers grew.

There, on the far side, three monsters were staring at them.

One was squat, hulking, and mud-colored. Another was tall and bony, with enormous clawed hands and feet. The third was the green thorny one like a walking tree, who had chased Melleron earlier.

Melleron whirled frantically around, looking for escape, but other fearsome shapes were looming at the sides of the glade. From behind he could hear the growls of Horrimal and his friends, closing in. Then, overhead, the winged catlike creature appeared, circling menacingly.

They were trapped, surrounded. Despair closed around Melleron's heart as he faced that final crushing defeat.

As he sagged, it was a last unbearable blow when yet another terrifying monster lumbered into the glade. It was the gigantic one he had seen before, with four arms and great tusks and long trailing yellow hair.

"What's all this?" the giant one boomed.

He wasn't looking at Melleron but at Rose and Grit. To his utter dazed amazement, Melleron saw that Grit was wagging his tail, while Rose, perched on a tall flower, was smiling.

"It's a long story, Chief," she said merrily, "but we're very glad to see you."

That was the moment when Horrimal and his five friends crashed into the glade, growling savagely, fangs bared at the sight of their victims standing in the open, as if giving up. Then Horrimal and company looked beyond the three

friends and saw the chief and the others, all around the glade, glaring at them.

Their growling stopped. Horrimal grunted in shock, some of his friends gulped or gasped, the small scaly one turned entirely white. Wheeling frantically, looking for escape, they halted again in new fright – as more big angry monsters barred the way.

The chief's scowl was terrifying. "You've caused enough trouble, Horrimal! I've put you in chains before, and I'll do so again! Take them away and bind them!"

Dejected and defeated, Horrimal and his gang were dragged away.

"Here's their magician friend," said a voice from above. The winged Orani floated to the ground – with a glitter-eyed swallow-hawk in her claws. "He doesn't seem to be able to fly..."

Suddenly the hawk shimmered and turned into Saelez again. Jerking away from Orani, hot-eyed and raging, he whipped out the sheaf of copied spells from his cloak and began to scream harsh words of terrible power.

CHAPTER 18

An End to Magic

Nothing happened at all.

As the monsters looked astonished, Orani gave a purring laugh. "It seems he can't do magic anymore, either."

"Um…" Melleron said, feeling a little nervous about speaking up. "His copies of spells are fading, so he can't say them properly. He doesn't have his spell-book, either."

"I'll find it!" Saelez shrieked. "You will all regret this when I do!"

"No," Melleron said, "you won't." Reaching into his shirt, he brought out the book.

Saelez screeched, in an even more towering fury. "Treacherous little thief!" he screamed. "You had it all along!" He flung himself at Melleron.

The monsters held him back, although he fought and howled and raged. The chief peered with interest at Melleron.

"You seem to be at the center of these adventures, young one," he boomed. "Most interesting, considering that you're the first human ever to set foot in our land."

"If it weren't for Melleron," Rose said pointedly, "Grit and I would be facing a horrible fate in Saelez's cave."

A ripple of shock and interest swept through the gathering of monsters. "That sounds like a story worth hearing, Rose," Poljon said with a thorny smile.

"You seem to be a most undesirable person, magician," the chief boomed, glaring at Saelez. "Something must be done about you. Perhaps if we destroy your magic book, that will put an end to your threat..."

Saelez cackled wildly. "You can't! The book is indestructible!"

Melleron sighed, knowing beyond doubt that the chief was right, that it had to be done. "No it isn't," he said. "A spell has appeared in the book, showing how to do it. It's difficult..."

"Then it will be far beyond you, fool of a boy!" Saelez yelled.

"Luckily," Melleron went on sharply, "it also showed a Swifter Way!"

Sudden fear silenced Saelez, as Melleron turned toward Rose.

"The Swifter Way to destroy the book is easy enough," he said, "but I need help to do it, from someone small and pink..."

Rose leaped into the air, in her berserk storm of fury at the hated word. "Not pink, not pink, not pink!" she shrieked, with blue fire exploding from her mouth.

Melleron threw the spell-book at her.

The stream of fire struck the book, enveloping it as it fell. All of them stared, even Rose, her fury forgotten. Instantly the blazing book shriveled into a cinder, then tore apart into tiny flakes of ash like black snow, drifting away across the glade, vanishing into nothingness.

"Sorry about having to say that, Rose," Melleron breathed, "but that's what was needed for the spell – dragon-fire."

Saelez was trembling and moaning, staring at his sheaf of papers – every one of which had gone completely blank. Flinging them aside, he turned with a crazed whimpering howl and staggered away into the brush.

"Let him go," the chief said hollowly. "He is no danger now."

"Then it's time to go home," Poljon said cheerfully.

"Indeed," the chief boomed, with a huge smile full of tusks. "It's also time to show Melleron a true monster celebration!"

Melleron blinked, taken aback. "Thank you," he said carefully, "but if you don't mind I'd like to start toward my home. It's such a long way, over the mountains…"

"Then let's celebrate right here!" Poljon suggested. "There's lots of food in the woods, and we wouldn't have to wait to hear Rose's story about all this!"

"Then I'll fly you home," Orani said to Melleron with a smile. "It'll take no time."

Melleron's eyes widened. "Won't Nan be amazed…" he breathed.

"She'll be too busy being thrilled to have you safely home," Rose said. "We'll come with you, if Orani doesn't mind carrying Grit as well. I think we want to stay in the Peaceful Forest for a while longer."

So all of them, Rose and Grit as well, rushed off to gather things to eat for the celebration. Melleron stayed in the glade, half-stunned with amazement and delight at how everything had so suddenly been turned around. Then, remembering, he reached into his shirt to look at the roll of birch-bark.

It was smooth and clean and totally blank. Not a letter, not the tiniest mark, remained of the spells he had written.

He sighed. So I won't be Melleron the Magician after all, he thought. Still, I was – for a time...

Smiling a wry smile, he tossed the bark aside, and went to join his friends.

About the Author

Whenever I finish a book, I feel sad. Leaving the people, the characters of the book, is like moving to a new house and leaving friends behind. When I finished a book about a boy and some  unusual creatures *(Melleron's Monsters)* I felt especially sad. I'd had such a good time with them, I didn't want to let them go.

So I decided to write another book about them. Although I'm a little sad again, now that I'm done, I know I can always go back and visit just as you can.

Douglas Hill